Write a Winning CV

D0266606

Write a
Winning CV

Julie-Ann Amos

howtobooks

DUDLEY PUBLIC LIBRARIES

1857038401

Askews	L 47730
331.128 Ci S	£6.99
Du	02.

Published by How To Books Ltd,
3 Newtec Place, Magdalen Road,
Oxford OX4 1RE, United Kingdom.
Tel: (01865) 793806. Fax: (01865) 248780
email: info@howtobooks.co.uk
http://www.howtobooks.co.uk

All rights reserved. No part of this work may be reproduced or stored in an information retrieval system (other than for purposes of review) without the express permission of the publisher in writing.

© **Copyright 2003 How To Books Ltd**

British Library Cataloguing in Publication Data.
A catalogue record for this book is available from the British Library.

Cover design by Baseline Arts Ltd, Oxford
Produced for How To Books by Deer Park Productions
Typeset by PDQ Typesetting, Newcastle-under-Lyme, Staffordshire
Printed and bound in Great Britain by Bell & Bain Ltd, Glasgow

NOTE: The material contained in this book is set out in good faith for general guidance and no liability can be accepted for loss or expense incurred as a result of relying in particular circumstances on statements made in the book. Laws and regulations are complex and liable to change, and readers should check the current position with the relevant authorities before making personal arrangements.

Contents

Preface

There is a vast amount of information available on how to write Curriculum Vitae. However, not all of it is helpful, and it may not be in line with what prospective employers want. Selecting the best advice for you can be difficult.

Employers want to see what you can offer; they want to see it presented quickly and simply. And they want to see it in a format that is good for them to process through their recruitment procedures.

A little research can not only make a CV look good, but can also make it pass quickly to the right person, getting you the opportunity to interview and make a personal impression.

A CV will not get you the job. It is designed to get you an interview, at which you can (a) show prospective employers why they should hire you, and (b) decide whether you really do want to work for them.

Julie-Ann Amos

Chapter 1

A Means to an End

In this Chapter:

♦ **knowing when to make a move**

♦ **knowing what you want**

♦ **identifying opportunities**

♦ **doing research and targeting employers.**

Before you write your CV, you need to know who your target audience is. Decide what you want before you write the document that will help you get it.

Unless you know where you're going, you'll never get there. It is vital that you sit down and get a definite idea of what job(s) you want and where to find them *before* you produce your CV.

Why? Because your CV is a means to an end. How do you know how best to sell yourself unless you know who you're selling to?

The best sales people find out who might want to buy their product, and why. They get to know both customers and potential customers, even people who might be able to introduce them to customers! Market research is big business.

Before you write your CV, do your own market research – it will enable you to write a far better one. The days when one CV suited everyone are over. **Targeting** your CV is one of the single most effective things you can do to get the right job. And the aim isn't just to get any job – it's to get you the best job possible.

Is this you?

- ❓ *I can't see why I need to keep adjusting my CV – how many ways are there to say what I've done?*

- ❓ *I've a lot of experience, and don't want to miss out on any opportunities, so shouldn't I make my CV as broad as possible so I don't restrict myself?*

- ❓ *I've been here a while and don't really know where to start looking for new job opportunities.*

- ❓ *There are so many job vacancies out there I get overwhelmed! How do I decide which ones to apply for?*

Knowing when to make a move

If you are not working, you are probably ready to start work on your CV already! But if you already have a job you need to give some thought to exactly when you should make a move to look for a new job.

If you need help deciding whether the time is right for you now, consider the following factors which may indicate your career could use a change:

- **Instability** – for example the possibility of redundancy or cost-cutting. If these may be on the cards, it would be just as well to start exploring your options in advance, just in case.

- **Interpersonal conflict** – you are no longer happy working with those you work with. Whilst if things become difficult with colleagues, it is tempting to think about leaving, don't be too hasty. Sometimes these things blow over given a little time. But then again, you have the right to feel happy and comfortable at work with your colleagues, and a fresh start can be good when necessary.

- **Lack of promotion prospects** – sometimes, it is unfortunately true that you need to move in order to progress. For example, if there are a large number of people in line for a particular promotion, or you are effectively 'blocked' by someone in the role above you being likely to stay there for some time (a so-called 'dead man's shoes' scenario). If there are no opportunities where you work, then a move may simply make good sense.

- **New boss or management** – changes in management can often mean changes – and maybe ones you disagree with! Or a new boss/manager coming in may not value your skills and input in the same way the old one did. Again, avoid hasty decisions and give both parties time to get to know each other, but if all else fails, maybe it is time to move on. Also, a new boss is unlikely to leave soon and thus create any career opportunities for progression!

- **No personal life** – if work is taking up so much time that you have no time for yourself, friends and/or family, it may be time to change roles.

- **Opportunity** – sometimes, the job market is right and there are more opportunities than at other times. In this situation, it makes sense to keep an eye out and investigate anything promising, rather than waiting for something to go wrong or prompt you to leave.

- **Poor performance** – this can often be a sign that your heart isn't in the job any more. Will a change of role make you feel better, more motivated? If so, this can make you do better work, and everyone likes to feel they are doing well. Sometimes a change really is as good as a rest.

- **Stuck in a rut** – as above, are you bored or stale in your current role? Will a change of role make you feel better, more motivated?

- **Salary** – if your salary is no longer adequate for your needs, or if others are being paid more in other organisations for the same type of work, you may need to move. There are many sources of salary information – from recruitment agencies, to job advertisements; even online salary surveys at some of the recruitment websites.

- **Technology** – if you are aware new technology is around which you don't get the chance to use, a move may be a good idea to keep up-to-date in your skills. Leaving it too long can be a bad thing, as you may fall behind the market in terms of the currency of your skills, and then find it harder to leave in the future. On the other extreme, if your employer is bringing in new technology you can't cope with, looking for a more familiar environment without the new technology can be better for you.

You never know when you might be made redundant, or unforeseen personal circumstances will force you to move! So keep your CV up to date at all times, and this will save you time and worry later if opportunity or necessity presents itself!

> *The best way to move is in your own time, at the best time. But keep the CV to hand and up to date at all times, just in case...*

Signs you need to update your CV include:

◆ Current role is not fully described.

◆ Changes of role since joining your current employer are not included.

◆ If you add your current job, your CV is flowing onto an extra page.

◆ You have included lots of personal hobbies and interests.

◆ You haven't recorded new software and technology introduced in the past few years.

◆ It doesn't show you as suitable for the type of roles you're now looking at.

◆ Contact numbers, faxes, e-mail addresses, etc. are not up to date.

Knowing what you want

So we have said you need to identify what you want before you start. You need a firm idea of what you're looking for in a new job, or you will waste time considering things that aren't right for you. You need to focus all your energy on getting the right job, not waste time thinking about lots of jobs that may or may not be suitable. Consider the following checklist:

Position:

◆ What type of work do you want to do?

◆ What type of company or organisation?

◆ What industry?

◆ Public or private sector?

◆ What department?

◆ Do you want to stay in your current field?

Salary:

◆ How important is it compared with other factors?

◆ How much would you ideally like to earn?

◆ Being realistic, what is the minimum you are prepared to accept?

◆ What benefits do you require – car, pension, healthcare, bonuses, etc?

Area/location:

◆ Where do you want to work?

◆ Where *can't* you work due to travel?

◆ How long are you prepared to spend travelling?

Other working conditions which are important to you:

◆ Office or working hours?

◆ Working with a team?

◆ Working alone?

◆ Flexible hours?

◆ A regular schedule?

◆ Casual dress?

◆ Learning/training opportunities?

◆ Promotion prospects?

◆ Travel opportunities?

Don't forget intangible factors

◆ Personal values and beliefs e.g. would you be happy working for a tobacco-related company? A company which produces chemicals?

◆ Self-employment – is this an option?

◆ A boss/manager you like and respect and can learn from?

♦ Good working atmosphere?

♦ Colleagues you can socialise with?

Early in their careers, people often make choices which are not especially good for them long term. Other people make financially-based choices rather than broadening their experience and skills. Take the time to make a long-term plan instead of moving job to job focusing only on the next move.

Identifying opportunities

Where do you look for a new job? Most people know the usual sources – the newspapers, job centres, recruitment agencies. But as the recruitment industry opens up, we are seeing more and more inventive ways of recruiting staff, and therefore more ways for potential candidates to find opportunities.

Know and use the recruitment methods available – don't be shy. But be careful – some methods will suit you better than others, so use the best methods for you.

Newspapers

♦ National papers for senior roles and jobs throughout the country.

♦ Local papers for local jobs.

- Don't forget papers such as FreeAds, etc., and any free 'through the door' papers in your area. These often have a large number of job advertisements.

Specialist publications

- Trade magazines, professional journals, etc.
- Usually have an 'Appointments' or 'Vacancies' section.

Job centres

- Still used by a lot of employers, but often offering less opportunities than some other sources.
- Jobs often go quickly.

Recruitment agencies

- Some specialise in certain industries or types of work, while others carry a wide variety of jobs.
- They have many vacancies they are trying to fill, and may also proactively market candidates to employers.
- Registering with them can hold you 'on file' against future openings, and can take some of the work out of looking for a job.
- Standards vary, and you will have to work to establish/maintain a relationship with the agency to get good results. This is because they often have large numbers of candidates on their books, and unless you are one of their more memorable candidates, it becomes a lottery whether you get good representation.

◆ They may take some of the work out of job-hunting, as they may assist you with preparing your CV – or even do it for you. This can be useful.

◆ Always ask for a copy of your CV for your records. You can then use this for your own job applications, but never assume it is the best format – don't be afraid to make a few changes if necessary.

Employment fairs

◆ Usually advertised in the local press.

◆ Recruitment agencies may hold them to increase their candidate pools.

◆ Companies may hold fairs or open evenings.

◆ Groups of employers may hold them together. For example, a recruitment agency may hold a fair and several different employers will participate, to try to attract new candidates.

Television

◆ There is a jobs page on teletext.

◆ Local job fairs may be advertised on teletext or local news programmes.

◆ Vacancies listings are sometimes shown on television in the early hours of the morning as an information service.

The Internet

If there is one single factor influencing the recruitment market today, it is the Internet. Growth of the Net has led to many new ways to find work.

◆ Recruitment websites ('job boards') which list vacancies only – such as Fish4Jobs, TAPS, etc.

◆ Recruitment websites ('CV banks') which you can post your CV onto, and employers look there for candidates when they have vacancies, such as Best of the Best, Planet Recruit.

◆ Websites which do both – e.g. Stepstone, Monster, Topjobs, Peoplebank, Totaljobs.

◆ Newspaper websites – most papers now have sites online which have an appointments section. Accessing the jobs this way can be quicker and easier than buying each paper daily. For example, *Telegraph, Evening Standard, Guardian,* etc.

◆ Local government websites usually have a vacancies section.

◆ There are many sites with a theme, e.g. local authority jobs, building jobs, secretarial jobs.

◆ Most recruitment agencies have sites, sometimes saving you the effort of going to the agency's offices.

◆ Companies often have their own websites, which may or may not have a 'Vacancies' or 'Jobs' section, and may even have the facility of applying for jobs online. This practice is increasing as technology advances.

Hints:

1 An internet search for 'vacancies' and 'jobs' will come up with thousands of possibilities. Try to be

more specific to narrow down the results to sites that will be most relevant to your needs.

2 When you find sites that are useful, use them thoroughly – there should be no need to keep looking for new sites if you are using the sites you *are* registered with effectively.

3 For a full explanation of internet job sites and how to apply online, *Job Hunt on the Net* (How To Books) covers this subject in more depth.

Advantages of using the Internet:

1 Most jobs can be applied for online.

2 Applying online saves you time and money.

3 It is a reliable way of ensuring your CV or application gets there in time.

Disadvantages:

1 Some sites have lengthy application processes. These are only worth spending time on if they have a reasonable turnover of jobs which you might want to apply for.

2 You need to keep an eye on how old the jobs are. Some boards hold out-of-date vacancies for quite long periods.

Doing research and targeting employers

It is still true to say that an awful lot of vacancies never get advertised anywhere. Therefore, if you know what you want to do, and have an idea of potential employers, it may be worth applying to them direct. The problem with this method is that it is rather like playing the Lottery. You have no idea whether they need anyone, so you will have to send an awful lot of applications to get a result – often up to 50 contacts to get one interview. But the companies will be ones you *know* you'd like to work for, so the end result may be worth it.

> *Be extra polite and careful – contacting companies direct is a bit of an unknown quantity. You don't know who will get your CV or how much your application will interrupt them.*

◆ Make a list of companies you like from job adverts – companies often paint a good picture of themselves in an advert, and you may really like the sound of them.

◆ Look at company websites. You can get a feel for the company this way.

◆ Ask people! Who have they worked for, and what were they like as an employer?

◆ Keep an eye on the news – who is growing – expanding their business?

◆ Are they a good company to go to?

◆ Do they have jobs in your field?

◆ What are their pay rates like?

◆ Where is the company going in the future?

Contacting potential employers

◆ Find out how and who to apply to, as stated previously. Try their website first, or look at job adverts they have placed.

◆ Failing this, call companies and ask who to address an application to. This is usually the head of the area you wish to work in, or the Personnel/HR department. Try to get a name to write to – it looks better. An e-mail address is ideal as it will save you time.

◆ *Always* keep it short and sweet – on the phone and in your application. They didn't ask you to contact them, so don't bother them more than necessary.

◆ Send a *short* (one side of paper max) covering letter with a copy of your CV, geared to the company and your relevance to the type of work within it that you want to do. You need to make your application relevant to that company in order for it to stand out and make any impression, given the number of speculative applications companies often receive.

◆ Tell them you're available, and make it clear what type of work you are looking for. If you are looking for any possible vacancies, say so.

◆ Ask them to contact you if your details are of interest.

◆ *Read* any response you get to your application. If it says don't apply again, don't. If it gives another route or method for applications (e.g. via their website, or via an agency), follow it.

◆ Keep records so you don't keep contacting the same companies by mistake. Repeat applications can do more harm than good!

In summary...

◆ Be brave enough to move at the right time, and always keep your CV up to date just in case.

◆ Save a lot of time and energy by identifying early on what you want and what you don't want.

◆ Use the full range of methods to find suitable opportunities.

◆ Research employers and apply direct if you wish .. but be aware this is a harder process.

Chapter 2

Presenting the Positive

In this Chapter:
- **the basics of presentation**
- **essential CV contents**
- **chronological format**
- **active writing**
- **functional format.**

Employers want to know what you've done, where you did it, and what you can do for them. There is no such thing as good enough – keep trying to improve your CV.

To produce a good CV, you need to make the most positive impression possible while being truthful. Giving false or misleading information may help you hide something negative on your CV, gain you an interview or even win you the job. But if discovered, it could also lead to dismissal.

A poor CV drones on and on about what you've done, when, how and why, even making excuses for what you *didn't* do. A good one gives an accurate sketch of your skills and experience. A job-winning one does this and also convinces the reader you're right for the job. And it convinces them in the face of sometimes hundreds, even thousands of other CVs competing for their attention.

To do this, it needs to be easy to read, attractive, and no longer than two or three sides of paper.

By design, you will see that all the example CVs in this book are different. This is because there is no one perfect way to set out your details: you should compare the different ideas and find one that best suits your own CV, and use that as a model layout.

Is this you?

❓ *I've been working for 20 years. I can't possibly get all that on to two sides!*

❓ *I'm worried I'll miss out the very thing that might land me the job if I edit it too much!*

❓ *All CVs are boring. Let's face it, mine isn't any different, and if it was it would look odd compared to everyone else.*

❓ *I haven't done anything especially outstanding, so how can I make it look good – it's a solid CV but*

❓ *I like it detailed – it shows everything I've done from start to finish. When I trim the CV down I lose too much detail.*

The basics of presentation

The general guidelines for producing a good-looking CV are simple.

♦ An overall look that grabs the attention and says 'LOOK AT ME!'

♦ A good layout that is clear and creates the best possible impression.

♦ Using the right format for the CV – chronological or functional.

♦ Interesting to look at.

♦ Worded using active descriptions.

♦ Accurately checked so there are no mistakes or 'typos'.

♦ A clear statement that leaves the reader in no doubt that you can actually do the job you are applying for.

♦ Covert references to the job description or advertisement – quoting words and phrases to re-emphasise that you fit their need.

The recruiter doesn't usually have time to read every word of every CV – so make sure that what they read of yours makes them want to read the rest of it.

There is a section in Chapter 5 on tailoring your CV to the job.

A good layout

◆ If printed, use good paper in white or cream. For the best impression, use quality, heavyweight paper – most stationers can advise.

◆ Don't make the CV look cramped – keep a reasonable amount of white space and borders.

◆ Make it easy to read.

The right layout

There are two main CV formats:

◆ chronological (your career history in date order)

◆ functional (by skills or experience).

Two very short one-page examples appear on the following pages to give you the basic idea, and the two formats are discussed in detail later in this chapter.

Interesting to look at

◆ Emphasise with bullet points, italic, bold text and capitals.

◆ Liven the CV up, but don't go overboard. Later you will see that CVs which are *not* going to be printed on paper, but sent electronically, need to be done *without* all these devices.

◆ Avoid gimmicks like coloured paper, text, snazzy envelopes and photographs.

JOHN JENKS

Flat 2 Lodge Road   TEL: 07999 123456 (Mobile)
1 Sydney Grove   020 7123 4567 (Home)
London NW1 42XE   EMAIL jjenks 23445@networks.com

DOB: 2 December 1976

EMPLOYMENT HISTORY
06/01-12/01:   J Rider Ltd, London
Position: Transaction Support Clerk
Duties: providing technical information, monitoring cash transactions

04/00-04/01:   Gillian Taylor Designs
Position: Sales Consultant and part-time Shop Manager
Duties: shop/telesales, customer service and bookkeeping

01/00-03/00:   Workfile Insurance
Position: Claims Administrator
Duties: recording claim details, implementing data entry, customer service

06/99-12/99:   John Soper Architects
Position: Project Administrator
Duties: liaising with clients/building manufacturers, and recording specifications

EDUCATION
- Foundation Diploma in Architecture Studies – London College of Design
- BTEC Foundation Diploma in Design – The Design College, London
- A-Levels: (grades A,B,B) Maths, Geography and Art & Design – Redvale 6th Form college
- GCSE's (8) – Redvale Boys School

SKILLS
- I.T.: MS Excel/Word/PowerPoint, desktop publishing and UNIX experience.
- Approximately 2 years database, customer service and administration skills.
- Languages: English and French (conversational).

Short example of chronological format

Jane Roper   07999-123456
22b Preston Close   Email Jroper@jroper.com
Exeter

EDUCATION:

1998 – 2001: **Exeter Business School**
             BA (Hons) Business Studies
             Winner: Patton Prize for Small Business
             2002

1996 – 1998: **Weybridge College, Exeter**
             A-Level Results: Maths (A), Geography (A),
             Accounting (C),

1992 – 1996: **Hawthornes Secondary School, Exeter**
             GCSE Results: 3 As, 6 Bs and 3 Cs

IT SKILLS: Familiarity with all of the Microsoft Suite: Access,
Excel, MS-DOS, PowerPoint, Publisher and Word.
Understanding and use of Lotus applications: 123, Notes,
Organiser and Ami Pro.

OTHER SKILLS:
Database skills   Moderate to advanced training received on
inputting and extracting relevant information.

Financial skills   Comprehensive interpretation of accounts
and a good knowledge and application of a variety of
accounting tools.

Leadership skills Participation in the Young Enterprise
Scheme, developed basic leadership and team-working skills.
Awarded responsibility of Managing Director.

Languages   FLAW (Foreign Languages at Work)
certificates at intermediate and advanced levels in German.
Translation of simple to moderate texts from German to
English and English to German. Can converse in German at
basic level.

Driving   Clean drivers licence held for five years.

HOLIDAY WORK:
Worked in family business on a variety of tasks – bookkeeping, administration, diary management, assisting with
order processing etc.

Short example of functional format

No mistakes

Advice on proofreading comes later. Suffice it to say that errors on CVs cost people jobs, because their applications often get screened out, and don't make it through to a stage where the CV is read thoroughly.

Active writing

♦ Avoid big words.

♦ Avoid management buzzwords.

♦ Keep descriptions simple and clear.

♦ Action words are best – they make it clear what you have been **doing**. Use active descriptions of what you *did*, not things that *were done*.

> *Don't get carried away. Employers are interested in your work, not your imagination or hairstyle.*

The general principle is to make the language and grammar used ACTIVE. This means wording sentences in a certain way, so that you talk about WHAT YOU DID – not about things that happened, what was done, events that took place. See the table opposite for some examples.

Not – responsible for cost control measures	*Use* – made savings of... by implementing cost controls
Not – manager of team of 5	*Use* – recruited, motivated, trained and managed team of 5
Not – secretarial support for Chief Executive	*Use* – provided confidential, professional, secretarial support service for Chief Executive
Not – accountant for company	*Use* – accountant – provided full financial services and accounting function for company

To get active language, take any words that are not active and change them. Here are some common words and their active formats.

Passive word examples:	Active format:
cost control	reduced and controlled costs
manager	managed
recruitment	recruited
savings achieved	achieved savings
provided support	supported
company research	researched companies
general administration duties	carried out general administration
stock reconciliations	reconciled stock
event management	managed and organised events

Can you see that one list is a list of *job functions*, and the other is a list of things you have *done*.

Essential contents

Whichever format of CV you choose, you should start with one sheet of paper (or half a sheet, as necessary) with basic information about yourself. This will be required whether using a chronological or functional CV.

Contact details

◆ **Name**.

◆ **Address**.

◆ **Telephone numbers**, plus mobile number if you have one. If you don't want them to leave a message at work, add 'no messages' after the work number, or do not quote a work number.

◆ **E-mail address.** Never give a work e-mail address. This implies you use your employer's e-mail for personal purposes, and prospective employers may either be concerned about approaching you at work, or may think it inappropriate for you to use your employers' e-mail in this way.

Qualifications

◆ **School examinations.** List them in full, with subjects if you have little or no experience. If you have work experience, just list the number of passes, saving space in the CV to write more relevant things.

There is no need to list every single examination you have ever taken. In particular, do NOT list exams you have failed. Better to show 5 passes than 5 passes and 2 failures.

If you have A levels, or a higher NVQ qualification, you can omit O level or GCSE grades. The general principal is only list the highest level of qualification grades you possess.

For example, if you have GCSE's only:

GCSE's:

Maths	B
English	B
Design	C
IT	B
Science	A

But if you have GCSE's and A levels:

A levels:

Maths	B
Chemistry	B
Geography	C

GCSE's:

Seven including Maths and English grade B

◆ **Professional qualifications.** Give the full name as well as the abbreviation form of letters, eg. Member, Institute of Personnel and Development (MIPD) – not just 'MIPD' – prospective employers may not know what they mean!

◆ **Degree or higher qualification.** Give the university or college. You don't have to give grades, but if you have a good grade, why not? Many employers are suspicious that if you don't list a degree grade, you have poor results, so if at all possible, include the grade.

◆ **Other qualifications.** Do not include 'other' qualifications, such as night classes, hobby-type courses, etc. unless they are relevant – for example, if you have little or no work experience, 'learning

French at evening class' may indicate that you are willing and able to be trained. However, a prospective employer doesn't need to know that you are studying Italian cookery!

'Good' other qualifications	*Irrelevant qualifications (unless appropriate to the job)*
Open university degree, 2 years completed	Certificate in car maintenance
Learning French at evening class	Taking evening classes in flower arranging
Taking correspondence course in accountancy	Diploma in art appreciation
Part qualified in basic first aid	

◆ **Failures**. Never mention any exams/courses failed. The only possible exception to this would be if you are left with a gap in your CV; for example, if you attended university for two years but then left without completing the course. You may then have to mention the course to avoid a conspicuous gap. If so, emphasise what you did do, not what you didn't – for example:

Not: University 1990–1992, left without completing degree

Say: Completed two years of BSc degree in Politics 1990–1992.

Other skills or experience

♦ Include relevant information that won't be highlighted in the main part of the CV, for example:

Cricket Club Treasurer	shows accounting ability
School Governor	shows responsibility, and awareness of educational issues

♦ Do not include references to personal websites unless they are professional in content and relevant to the job. They will rarely help you get a job unless you are in advertising, marketing, art, design, etc.

If you have anything that may help your CV that doesn't fit logically elsewhere, create an 'other' skills or 'experience' section.

Hobbies and interests

Avoid mentioning hobbies or interests unless they are relevant and say something about your skills and abilities. It is true that some employers still look for hobbies and interests, to see that you do have some form of life outside work! But keep them as short as possible to avoid taking up too much space; one line is ideal. If, however, you can use a hobby or interest to promote some skill or experience you have, here is a good chance. For example:

Badminton Team Match Co-ordinator – arrange transport, fees and venue bookings for all club matches.

Women's Institute Summer Fête Organiser – co-ordinated and supervised all aspects of this annual event.

References

Never include these. Give them when asked for later. Some unscrupulous recruitment agencies have been known to approach them as possible candidates! It's a matter of personal taste, but there is little point in saying 'References available on request', because nowadays virtually all employers routinely check references. You will almost certainly be asked for them anyway, so don't bother saying you have them available.

Type of work sought

Never write a paragraph about what you're looking for. Most employers don't care – what they care about is what *they're* looking for. Use the space to convince them it's you! Rather than a paragraph about your goals or aspirations, use a paragraph to summarise you!

Summary of yourself

It's becoming common to see a short paragraph summarising yourself. This, however, is NOT essential, so it's a matter of personal taste if you wish to include this.
This is what I call the 'ten second sales pitch' – the

section to get the employer's attention and persuade them to read the rest of the CV. This is especially relevant if you have little or no work experience to refer to.

> *Any summary of yourself goes on the front page. It's like the 'blurb' on the back of a book – when you glance at it, it needs to grab your attention and persuade you to buy it and read it.*

Here are some examples:

> Management Honours graduate with practical (holiday and part-time) work experience in various manufacturing companies. Projects include managing working teams and presenting group findings to management.

> A self motivated, confident and enthusiastic college leaver. Enthusiastic to learn and undertake new challenges.

> A very focused individual with a proactive outlook. A good team player with a meticulous and diligent approach to work. Works well under pressure and is capable of identifying inventive solutions to problems. Technically literate with strong IT skills.

> An accurate, efficient secretary with an eye for detail. Professional in both manner and presentation. Works well both as an individual and as part of a team.

A competent and conscientious Administrator with excellent organisational skills and skilled in dealing with problems in a resourceful manner. Good communicator who enjoys developing effective working relationships, used to working in a team whilst very capable of utilising own initiative. Competent in using Word and Excel computer packages.

A responsible team leader with excellent communication and interpersonal skills. Produces quality work under time constraints. Enthusiastic, reliable, committed and self-motivated with the determination to complete all tasks to best ability.

Chronological format

This is arranging your CV in date order. The correct way to do this is actually in reverse order – starting with the present and working backwards in time to your first job. Never start with your first job and work towards the present, as most employers find this really confusing. Also, it would mean that you would probably be listing the most relevant experience last which is not helpful if your CV only gets a quick glance!

Most employers prefer this format, as they can easily see your work record at a glance. On the following pages you will see an example of a typical chronological CV. There are further examples in the Appendix starting on page 83.

List job title

Where this is ambiguous or doesn't accurately reflect your actual role, change it or explain in brackets. For example:

Not – Team Leader

Use – Leader/Manager of Administration Team

Or – Team Leader (managing Administration Team of five staff)

List the employer

Where the company has been sold, merged, taken over or changed name, show this clearly. For example:

XXX company (now YYY corporation)

Give duties and achievements for each job

Use active language that describes what it was you actually did.

◆ Describe achievements in terms people can easily understand, especially if your industry uses a lot of jargon/technical terms, or your experience was military. Imagine you are explaining to a small child. Then make the same information sound interesting and impressive to an adult.

◆ If possible use words that make your job experience and achievements fit the job you are applying for.

◆ If you have an advertisement or job description to refer to, ensure you use the same language as is used on that. This will maximise your chances of being perceived to be a good fit with their requirements.

List dates
List dates (to the nearest month) for each job. For example:

> January 1997 – March 1999

Gaps
If you have short gaps between your jobs, you can cover these by listing the year rather than month. For example:

Not   January 1995 – March 1996

June 1996 – October 1998

Use   January 1995 – early 1996

Early 1996 – October 1998

Use chronological format when you have:

◆ a sequence of relevant jobs, moving upwards

◆ relevant experience in the type of work

◆ continuous work history, or work history with only short gaps.

Chronological CVs are easy to read and understand. They work well for most people.

33

ANGELA MADDING
7 Harrington Drive, Middlesborough, MB3 45G,
Tel: 0777 999 5555

A reliable, confident, multi-lingual individual with outstanding leadership, organisational and time-management expertise. Ability to work on own initiative plus excellent communication and interpersonal skills.

Sept 01 – Present   **PA TO DIRECTOR/PA TO CEO**
Morris Fund Management – London

Feb 98 – Aug 01   **PA TO BOARD DIRECTOR (Multi-lingual)**
Initial Indemnity – Canary Wharf, London
- Minute-taking and preparing presentations (PowerPoint)
- Organising events and conferences/diary management
- Correspondence in French and Spanish (including dictation)
- Dealing with highly confidential issues as necessary
- Organising extensive travel itineraries
- Liaising with VIPs, organising hotels and chauffeurs
- Created new office filing/archiving system/holiday records
- Company Secretary to Sports and Social Committee
- First Aider and Fire Marshal

March 97 – Feb 98   **PA TO DIRECTOR**
Arabian Astra Corporation – London
- Minute-taking, conference and travel organising
- Dictation, dealing with confidential issues
- Diary management

Sept 96 – March 97   **PA TO DIRECTOR**
WTN Ltd – London NW1
- Organising complex event and travel itineraries
- Diary management
- Planning conferences

Example of a chronological CV (page 1 of 2)

April 95 – Aug 96	**RESORT MANAGER**
	Springview Holidays - Alicante

- ◆ Full office management using Spanish and French
- ◆ Organising exotic weddings
- ◆ Events and conference organising
- ◆ Marketing and advertising
- ◆ Setting up new Spanish office
- ◆ Solely responsible for incoming guests (500 per week)
- ◆ Managing and motivating a team
- ◆ Implementing sales targets and incentives

Jan 92 – March 95	**PUBLIC RELATIONS MANAGER**
	Faversham Hotel – Alicante

- ◆ Multi-lingual Office Manager/PA role using Spanish and French
- ◆ Marketing and research for new events
- ◆ Responsible for all day and night activities in the complex including planning and compering for entertainment, fashion shows and live bands

March 90 – Jan 92	**CONFERENCE MANAGER**
	Bluewave Hotel Truro

- ◆ Managing conference centre and all bookings
- ◆ Promotion of events and marketing for new business
- ◆ Responsible for conference administrator

LANGUAGES	Fluent French and Spanish (bilingual) basic German
SHORTHAND	80 wpm
TYPING	50 wpm
COMPUTER SKILLS	Windows 95-98, Adv. Microsoft Outlook, PowerPoint, Excel, Lotus Notes
EDUCATION	Eastbourne Technical College
	3 'A' levels: English, French and Spanish
	Institute of Linguists/Distinction in Spanish
	Eastbourne C of E School
	8 'O' levels
HOBBIES	Latin American dancing (club secretary), and kick-boxing

Example of a chronological CV (page 2 of 2)

Be warned that:

◆ Gaps in your CV (i.e. time between jobs) will show unless you deliberately avoid this, and to some extent, it's dishonest to deliberately hide them.

◆ Periods of unemployment will be highlighted.

◆ Moves sideways or demotions will be highlighted.

◆ If you have no work experience or no relevant experience, this format will *not* sell you well.

Functional format

This is a useful format to use in situations where you don't have a track record of jobs to list. For example, where you are a school, college or university leaver. A sample CV in functional format can be found on the following pages. There are further examples at the back of the book.

Use functional format when you have:

◆ no work experience (e.g. school or university leavers)

◆ no relevant experience (e.g. changing jobs completely, returning to work after children, etc.)

◆ been travelling overseas

◆ worked freelance, consulting or self-employed

◆ been unemployed for some time

◆ been a full-time parent for a while

◆ job-hopped

- only worked for one employer but had a variety of different jobs – it can make more sense than a chronological CV

- something to hide on the CV (think twice – employers aren't stupid; they may well see through this)

- emphasise your skills and achievements as they relate to the job in question

- remember that other responsibilities outside your main job – such as running clubs, social teams, managing playgroups, barrack blocks, etc. – may give you just as much relevant experience as your main job – sometimes more

- to decide what headings to use for your groupings, read the advert or job description and pick out key areas they require, then add areas to cover all your 'selling points'. For example:

  Management experience
  Communication skills
  Budgeting
  IT skills
  Projects worked on
  Teaching experience
  Areas of responsibility
  Staff supervisory experience
  Courses included
  Points learned

- Concentrate on what you *can* offer. Don't make excuses or suggest how you can overcome what you

MARTIN HOBSON

Martin House, Derby (01725) 123456 –
mh314676@hotmail.co.uk
Date of Birth: 13/01/1979 – Nationality: British

PERSONAL STATEMENT

Extremely hard-working, efficient and dedicated. Can adapt
to different types of challenge, whether as part of a team, or
individual. First class honours degree in French from Channing
College, London.

ACADEMIC ACHIEVEMENTS

Blackwell-Boyne Prize for Outstanding Achievement in Final
Year Modern Languages programme at College.
Dean's Prize for the Best Overall First Year Student on the
Languages honours programme at College.

POSITIONS OF RESPONSIBILITY HELD

President of College French Society, 1999–2000:
Organised conference for 250 students from assorted colleges
and universities.

**Treasurer and Social Secretary Chairman of College Karate
Club, 1999–2000:**
Organised club finances and social events.
Responsible for all funds and solvency of club.

**Managing Director of School Young Enterprise Company
1995–6**
Responsible for team of 6 classmates.
Ultimate decision-making for Company.
Chairing and organising all meetings.
Co-ordinating all company activity.

Treasurer of School Football Club – 1994–7
Elected to manage the club's funds and responsible for
receiving and disbursing the club's revenue.

Example of a functional format CV (page 1 of 2)

Created and monitored ledger account and income and expenditure account.

At club meetings, responsible for making recommendations on future expenditure to the club's committee.

SKILLS AND ABILITIES
Management Skills:
- Managed conference and volunteers for French society.
- Organised social events for Karate Club.
- Managed team for Young Enterprise company – elected MD.

Financial Skills:
- Solely responsible for Karate Club Finances (Treasurer) 130 members, turnover approx £25,000 per annum.
- School Football Club Treasurer responsible to headmaster for solvency of team, including sponsorship raising and kit purchasing.

Time Management and Organisational Skills:
- Planned and organised conferences and social events for college clubs as above.
- Time management of resources to accommodate both extra-curricular activities and academic studies.
- Managed personal time to achieve academic excellence whilst maintaining commitments to clubs and societies.

Interpersonal Skills:
- Negotiated and purchased kit and supplies for sports clubs.
- Chaired meetings and managed Young Enterprise company.
- Negotiated assistance and volunteers to run French Society conference, involving 32 volunteers and guest speakers.

Example of a functional format CV (page 2 of 2)

can't offer an employer. Never say 'willing to learn' or 'open to training'. If you do want to say something, say 'intelligent' or 'learns quickly'.

◆ Highlight anything you have done to prepare yourself for your new career – training, research, voluntary work, etc.

Be warned that:

◆ Employers may be suspicious you have something to hide with this format of CV.

◆ This format will highlight any 'fit' between your skills and/or experience and the job, so if you don't know what they are looking for, it's hard to sell yourself well.

◆ An employer isn't going to translate a CV if they don't understand the language. So write it so they can understand exactly what you have to offer.

Some employers are suspicious if they do not see chronological format.

In summary...

◆ Make your CV say 'READ ME!!!'

◆ Make the first page especially clear, concise and attractive.

◆ Use the best format CV to fit your situation, and always make it fit the job.

◆ Use language the employer will understand.

Chapter 3

Avoiding any Negatives

In this Chapter:
◆ **lack of track record**
◆ **lack of qualifications or education**
◆ **technical problems and gaps**
◆ **too much experience or qualifications.**

No one has a perfect CV, but there's no need to put in a section that says 'DON'T HIRE ME!'

Most of us have something on our CV we don't feel makes us look good. The trick isn't to hide it, and be dishonest. Instead, reduce it, or even use it to your advantage. Accentuate the positive, as seen in the last section, and tone down the negative, so it is seen as less important. Use weaknesses to your advantage by making them relevant.

Even good things can be a negative if put in a clumsy way. Too much can be as bad as too little experience. Too many qualifications may put people off. Good skills may make people think you will grow out of the job too quickly.

On the other hand, weaknesses can be made to look interesting. Remember that you should tailor your CV to suit the job; each weakness should be checked to ensure it shows you in the best possible light.

Is this you?

❓ *I haven't the experience or skills for this job. There's no point trying.*

❓ *It's all very well until they see that on my CV, then I've blown it.*

❓ *I have nothing to hide. If they don't like it, they don't have to hire me.*

❓ *I know it's a bit dishonest, but I figure if I can get the interview, then I can explain it then, and if they like me, maybe it won't matter. So I tend to leave out the bad bits!*

❓ *Finding out problems is the interviewer's job. What they don't find out is their responsibility. Why should I tell them the worst, and run the risk of not getting the job?*

Honesty vs dishonesty

Before we discuss how to handle any negative aspects of your CV, always remember that employers will never want to hire a dishonest person. Whilst the following pages may assist you in 'cleaning up' any trouble spots on your CV, it is not advised that you deceive future employers. Many employment contracts or terms and conditions of employment make a specific provision for dismissing dishonest employees, so if found out, you stand to lose the job you worked so hard to get anyway!

Lack of track record

We don't all have a track record of relevant experience to sell us to potential employers.

> *If you don't have past experience, you need to show future potential. That's what will get you the job in this situation.*

No work experience – first job

◆ Try to get some, even if it is temporary or unpaid. This will enhance your CV and stand you in good stead for future opportunities.

◆ Focus on skills you have which you *could* use at work.

◆ Refer to summer jobs, evening or weekend work, and work placements/work experience programmes you may have done.

◆ Refer to projects and subjects studied which show you know what is required.

◆ Present your youth as an advantage – it makes you keen to progress, willing to learn, and used to training.

No relevant experience – changing career track

◆ Why not try to get some experience – unpaid, part-time if necessary? Again, this would stand you in good stead for the future.

◆ Make sure you state on the covering letter *why* you are changing career so it makes sense to the employer. Otherwise, employers can sometimes be negative about career changes.

◆ Make your reasons positive not negative.

    e.g.   Keen to join the IT industry due to growth potential and the challenge of new technology, which I find stimulating.

    not   Stale in current role, and looking for more interesting work.

◆ Ex-military people need to phrase their experience appropriately – *not* in military words, but in simple language emphasising the skills and responsibilities that were relevant.

◆ Making your past experience sound relevant, although it may be different, is paramount.

Hints

◆ Don't focus on the job description or advertisement initially. That will highlight to you the areas you are weak in. Start with a list of skills you *do* have, and then see how these can fit the job description or advert.

- Be open and honest. You can't hide lack of track record on your CV, so put it positively.

- Use volunteer and unpaid experience if you can.

- Describe coursework or projects or subjects covered in education if relevant.

- Consider a functional CV format to highlight your skills as you have no track record to use. This is your only real option to make a professional looking CV.

- You may need to consider taking a lesser position, or one with less desirable conditions, in order to gain experience and then try to gain a more appropriate role in, say, six months. For example, saying 'willing to work shifts or weekends' in a covering letter may open up possibilities.

Lack of qualifications or education

Awaiting qualifications

- List the qualifications and state 'pending results' after them instead of grades.

Midway through a course

- List the course and when you expect to finish it, for example:

    NVQ Level III in Office Administration, completion expected September 2001

- If you have an idea of likely grades, you can give them – but it is unlikely to impress – after all, anyone can predict they will do well. If you have grounds for expecting a particular grade, then it makes sense to say so. For example:

2.1 expected based on coursework grades to date.

Qualifications from another country

◆ State not only the qualification, but what it is equivalent to in this country whenever possible.

◆ Make it easy for the employer. If they haven't heard of your qualification(s), you run the risk that they may discount them.

No qualifications

◆ If you studied but gained no qualifications – for example, if you left school without any – you could put your attendance down. Simply list the establishment and the dates you attended.

◆ If you have work experience to present, just omit the section on education – after all, you have experience instead.

Hints

◆ Focus on experience.

◆ Don't highlight what you are lacking – play it down.

◆ Make it easy for an employer to see you have the skills even though you may not have the qualifications.

◆ Have you considered taking some qualifications?
Evening classes are available at relatively low cost,
and you can take GCSEs, certificates, NVQs, etc.

*The lucky people have experience **and** good
qualifications. If you are missing one, accentuate the
other.*

Technical problems and gaps

Returning to work after a break or gap

◆ Why did you have a break? Employers will sadly
often discount CVs with unexplained gaps in them if
they have quality CVs from people with no gaps. This
may be unfair, but it's a fact of life. In order to
compete, if there is a gap that you need to show,
explain it as positively as possible.

◆ Does an employer really need to know? If you can
construct the CV without a gap being obvious, you
could try this. It will need to be disclosed at some
point, but it may get you as far as an interview, so
you have your chance to progress.

Periods of unemployment

◆ State the date you left your last job, and never leave a
blank between then and now. State from that date to
present and say something about what you have been

doing – even if it was raising a family, travelling, etc.

♦ List training and other activities you have been occupying yourself with. Basically, you need to reassure employers you haven't been sitting around doing nothing.

♦ Never lie and try to hide the break unless it is very short – say, eight weeks or less. Many employers now check and you could be dismissed if it is later discovered that you have falsified your CV.

Raising a family

♦ Having children isn't a crime. Don't hide it as if it were. For example:

1993–1996 Full-time parent

♦ Gaps in your CV need careful handling to draw attention away from them without dishonesty.

You quit your last job

♦ This is a tricky situation, as you need to reassure employers you had a good reason, and won't do it to them!

♦ If there has been a short gap, don't mention it yet.

♦ State the date you left, and say something positive, for example:

left of own volition
resigned for personal reasons

immediately available

◆ Always be prepared to explain in depth at an interview.

Criminal records

◆ Some criminal offences have to be disclosed if you are asked for them. But don't offer them if not asked.

◆ Even disclosable offences may eventually become 'spent' after a certain period of time and you no longer have to mention them when asked.

◆ Check the status of your convictions – disclosable or not, when they become spent, etc.

I was fired

◆ Don't ever state this. Even if it is true, you don't need to put it on your CV, where it will probably prevent you from being interviewed. Leave it out, and be prepared to both disclose this and explain, but at a later stage.

◆ If asked at interview, you can explain then.

◆ If it will appear on a reference, let the employer know *after* they have offered you the job but before they get the reference.

◆ If you were fired from your last job and are now looking after a gap, simply state the date you left and 'reasons to be discussed at interview'. If the gap is short enough, don't mention it.

Hints

◆ Cover reasons for breaks, etc. positively in your covering letter.

◆ Be positive and unapologetic about what you *did* do during any break.

◆ *Never* give reasons for leaving unless you have left your last job and there has been a gap long enough that you need to mention it. For past roles, never state why you left.

◆ Don't let things stand in the way of what you can do. A lot of things are best left until later in the recruitment process, and aren't matters for the CV.

◆ Nobody is advocating that you lie. But keep sticky subjects until later once you have had the chance to prove yourself.

Too much experience or qualifications

◆ Strange though it may sound, having **too much** experience or too many qualifications can be a problem.

◆ This usually arises when older or more experienced candidates have more to show on their CV, simply because they have been around a lot longer.

◆ A major reason for rejecting a candidate can be that they are 'overqualified' or 'over-experienced'. This is because employers fear that if they are so well qualified or experienced, they will get bored with the role quickly and wish to move on – and generally speaking when an employer hires someone, they like them to stay for a reasonable period of time.

> *Too much can be as off-putting as too little. Employers don't want to feel threatened. Word things carefully.*

Age

◆ Don't set yourself up for age discrimination. Unfortunately, it does happen.

◆ The older you are, the more experience you have to show. Only list the last ten years or so. Head the section 'Recent Experience' so it isn't dishonest and made to look as though that were *all* your experience.

◆ Use careful wording.
    e.g.   more than ten years' experience
    not   26 years' experience.

◆ The older you are, the less relevant your qualifications may be. Consider omitting them if you have a wealth of experience instead.

◆ You do not need to put your age or date of birth on a CV.

◆ You do not need to show the date of qualifications – if you are mature and they were taken some time ago, don't even list your education, just give a bullet point list of qualifications without dates.

Lots of short jobs

◆ This is commonly known as job-hopping and usually regarded as a negative thing by many employers.

◆ The only time when this isn't likely to be viewed as negative is if you have specialist skills, or have been contracting or temping.

◆ Bundle together lots of short jobs to make a meaningful period of time, for example:

> administrative work, various companies

◆ Leave out some small entries if they're less than, say, a month, and wouldn't be missed.

◆ Combine several jobs under one heading, for example:

> residential care worker, ABC, DEF, GHI
> and JKL companies.

Being overqualified

◆ Give your reasons for wanting the job in the covering letter, quite clearly and positively.

◆ Never say you've resorted to a lesser job in lieu of a better one – even if it's true. Find a positive slant.

◆ Let the employer know that you are aware you're overqualified without being patronising in any way.

◆ You could 'play down' your experience so it looks less as though you *are* overqualified. But this will preclude you from any other more appropriate vacancies they might have coming up. It would be a shame to play down your experience and get the job, but miss out on a more senior one that was coming up.

◆ You certainly don't have to list all your qualifications if it isn't to your advantage.

Worked at one company for a very long time

◆ List each role you have held separately, as if you had moved companies with each new job.

◆ Emphasise outside experience and knowledge where possible.

◆ Emphasise job progression.

◆ Explain in your covering letter why you are looking to move *now*, after all this time.

◆ Be aware that some employers may be suspicious of whether you will make the adjustment to a new company successfully. Be sensitive to this and use words and phrases throughout the CV that emphasise your ability and enthusiasm for change.

In summary...

◆ Emphasise what you *do* have going for you, and play down what you haven't.

◆ Never try to create an academic background – just work with what little you have.

◆ A gap in your employment history isn't the end of the world – if you explain it so employers aren't suspicious.

◆ If you have too much experience or are overqualified, play things down so as not to threaten employers.

Chapter 4

The Covering Letter

In this Chapter:
- **the basics**
- **getting noticed**
- **targeting the company**
- **disclosing your salary.**

A good covering letter will literally *cover* any problem areas and complex issues and explain them – thus making the CV more likely to be read.

Covering letters introduce your CV. They are there to induce the reader to go on and read the CV, and to explain away any 'difficult' areas in the CV that might otherwise be off-putting.

They tell the reader why you want the job, why they should interview you, and that you are available. A good covering letter will make the impression that your CV is a good one, and that you are therefore an excellent candidate. It allows you the room to explain anything that isn't obvious, that needs clarification, etc.

If the CV is a sales pitch for yourself, the covering letter is a sales pitch for the CV. The CV is a tool to get you an interview, and the covering letter a tool to get the CV noticed for the right reasons. Preparing a good, personalised covering letter takes time, but it is a worthwhile investment.

Is this you?

❓ *I never know what to say – surely the CV should be enough?*

❓ *I send my CV by e-mail mainly. Surely I don't need a covering letter then – I usually just say it's attached.*

❓ *If I add a covering letter that's another page. I've heard you should make your applications as short as possible. So which is it?*

❓ *I don't like writing covering letters – they seem too friendly and I don't even know the person. Surely I should be more professional until we've at least met?*

The basics

The basics of any covering letter are the same as any other important letter. Just bear in mind the importance of this particular letter: if you get it right, you might get a CV looked at that wouldn't otherwise have been. If you get it wrong, you may stop your excellent CV from being considered.

> *Keep the covering letter simple, short and looking good.*

Covering letters are especially important if you are applying speculatively to a company, i.e. not in response to a known vacancy. In this instance, they have to clearly state why you're writing to them, and give the reader a real reason to look at your CV.

- **Include your name, address and contact numbers**. Even if they are on the CV.

- **Address personally**. Find out the right person's name, how to spell it, and then use it. Never try to address a covering letter to a job title.

- **Follow instructions**. If an advertisement says write to a particular person, do it. If it says quote a reference, quote it in the title of your letter. Some organisations may have recruitment policies that disqualify anyone not following the instructions given, **so follow the instructions!**

- **Choose a good title**. If there is a reference to be quoted, use the job title and the reference, for example:

    Senior buyer – Reference QC4758

    If there is no reference, use the job title and the place and date you found the advertisement, for example:

    Senior Accounts Clerk – Evening Standard

17 January 200X

- **Make it obvious**. Put the title in bold, underlining if it looks right. The recruiter may have several different vacancies and needs to see quickly which you are applying for.

- **Be professional**. Use good quality paper and neat typeface. If sending an e-mail application, keep it businesslike.

- **Stick to the point**. The letter is to introduce the main thing – your CV. It should never be longer than one side of paper.

- **Avoid gimmicks**. Coloured paper, fancy lettering, gold signatures, etc. may all get you noticed, but for the wrong reasons. Remember the basics – white or cream paper only.

- **If you really want to make a quality impression**, use an A4 card-backed envelope. This prevents your letter and CV from being folded or creased in the post, and it will arrive in as perfect condition as it is sent. It is surprising how many people print off a beautiful, pristine CV and then fold it and squash it into a small envelope...

- **Avoid unavailability**. Try not to state when you *aren't* available for interview – unless you will be away some time, for example, on holiday. Employers like to see you at their convenience, not yours! If they want to see you, you can discuss when you can and can't make it at that stage.

- **Write well**. Get help if necessary. Short words, short

sentences, short paragraphs, good English. Avoid jargon.

◆ **Refer to the CV**. After all, the idea is to get them to read it...

◆ A clear elegant covering letter can get a mediocre CV noticed.

Getting noticed

The basics are all very well, but how do you decide what else to put in a covering letter? How do you make an impression? Remember, there may be hundreds of applications arriving with yours, so how do you make yours one of the ones selected?

◆ **Show interest**. It's surprising how many covering letters don't actually say they want the job. Show you're interested.

　　e.g.　　I was extremely interested to see your advertisement for the above position.

　　or　　I think this would be an exciting opportunity.

◆ **Clear up problem areas**. Clear up anything in the CV that is ambiguous, or needs explaining, clearly and concisely. Don't be apologetic.

◆ **Put yourself forward**. Don't be shy. If you can, pick out some skills or experience they are looking for that you have, and mention it here. Give them a reason to choose you over other candidates.

　　e.g.　　I have three years' experience in a similar

role, and am now ready for the greater responsibility offered by this post.

◆ **Give a reason for applying**.

e.g.   I have been interested in technology for some time, and would welcome an opportunity to move into a more progressive environment.

◆ **Flatter them – but carefully**. There's nothing wrong with a little flattery – so long as you don't overdo it. Mention things you like about their company if relevant. But DON'T go on and on about it. Too much is worse than nothing.

e.g.   I have always been interested in your innovative marketing, and would like to join a team working with such success in developing new ideas.

◆ **Don't grovel**. It's surprising how many candidates adopt a 'please, please consider me, if it's not too much trouble' attitude. It makes you look as if you are desperate for the job, and lacking in confidence. Take the position that you want the job, you're right for it, and they *should* be looking at you. Be confident enough that it shows.

◆ **Don't repeat the CV**. Give *new* information. The covering letter is an opportunity to show 'soft skills' that may not come across in your CV, such as interpersonal skills, teamwork, maturity, etc.

◆ Keep it short. One side of A4 is quite sufficient. You don't need 2 pages, and many recruiters won't reach that much anyway.

Your covering letter may not even be read, but it's a good chance to try to get yourself noticed. Anyone can write a 'standard' covering letter, copied from a book. Yours should make an impression.

Targeting the company

In order to get noticed, you need to know something about the company. You will have learned something from the advertisement if you are responding to one.

There is a section in Chapter 5 on analysing the advert or job description for useful information. You will also need to do some research into the company – from the Internet, recruitment agencies, etc. The name of the game is to say not just 'I read your advert' but that I know who you are, what you do, and I'd like to be part of the team. I have what you want, and I'd like to join you.

Here are some hints as to how to find out about a company that has a vacancy you would like to apply for.

Finding out information

◆ Look for other advertisements they may have, which may say more about them. Add together the images gained to get a picture of the company.

◆ Search on the Internet for their website.

◆ Search the Internet for instances where their company is listed on other websites, e.g. recruitment agency sites, job boards, etc.

◆ Look through their company literature – they may send you some if you call and ask them for it, and this can be a good source of information.

◆ Ask people if they know anyone who works there and then talk to them.

◆ Check business journals and papers.

◆ Phone recruitment agencies and ask if they deal with the company. If you find one that does, say you might be interested in making a move to join that company, and ask what they can tell you about the company and any vacancies.

How to target your letter

◆ **News.** Refer to any recent news, e.g. office relocation, a product launch, a merger, new advertising.

◆ **What they do.** Refer to what they do, to show you understand what the company is about.

◆ **Why them?** Tell them why you like the idea of working for them, rather than one of their competitors (no need to mention names).

    e.g.   Your products are more user-friendly than others available.

    or   Your reputation as a leading developer within the industry...

◆ **Match your skills and CV to their requirements**. If
you know they are a young, growing company, make
yourself sound keen and enthusiastic. If you know
they are an established family firm, sound mature
and professional. Chapter 5 shows how to do this.

◆ **People you know**. Now, this is a matter for careful
thought. Referring to people you know at the
company may be a good thing, or it may cause
resentment if the recruiter thinks you are trying to
use an unfair advantage. How would you feel if you
were recruiting someone to work with you, and an
applicant said they knew your boss? You might feel
obliged to see that person, but might feel badly that
you were forced to. If, on the other hand, you heard
about the job in conversation with someone, you
might want to refer to this. If you have a contact who
has perhaps worked with you before and would be
willing to speak highly of you, it is sometimes worth
mentioning that they suggested you apply. But always
let them know you are doing this, and check they are
happy for you to do so.

e.g.   I met Mr Dawson at a conference last week,
       and he mentioned that you might be looking
       for a new Warehouse Supervisor. As he knows
       the standard of my work from a previous
       mutual employer, he suggested I might make a
       suitable applicant, so I enclose my CV for your
       consideration.

Disclosing your salary

It is virtually never in your best interests to disclose your salary – unless you think that the role you are applying may pay less than you currently earn or require, and so you can avoid going through pointless interviews.

Some employers ask for 'full salary history'. This is usually irrelevant, and this is one exception to the 'follow instructions' rule.

> *Giving your salary is almost never to your advantage. Unscrupulous employers may use it to reduce the salary for the role, or even misjudge your capabilities – or not bother to judge them at all.*

◆ Only give your current or last salary at most.

◆ Never disclose salary unless asked for it.

◆ If asked for it, it goes in the covering letter, not the CV.

◆ Only state current salary, or last salary if not currently working.

◆ You don't have to give it just because they ask for it!

The following advice is given assuming you have been asked to state your current salary, and feel that you should do so.

Salary is high compared to the role you seek

You would think an employer would be lucky to get someone willing to take a pay cut to work for them, wouldn't you? After all, wouldn't it be ideal to get someone just right for the job, but better than necessary? No. It often makes employers suspicious, particularly as they may think you are only taking the role as a temporary measure, and will move on as soon as something better comes up. They may also think you will have unrealistic promotion expectations.

Ways around the problem:

- If willing to take a pay cut, say so.

- Always explain why.

- Add a reassuring sentence, to ensure they know that this would not just be a 'stop gap' and that you would stay in the role.

- List the salary in as 'played down' a form as you can – just list basic salary, without bonuses, overtime, etc. and don't mention any extra cash or benefits you get.

- Omit the salary – although you run the risk of your application being discounted, many employers won't do this. If you are sending out a number of applications, why not try it?

Salary is low compared to the role you seek

Nowadays, there is an expectation that we will better ourselves when we change jobs. So employers typically expect to see someone looking for a modest salary increase. But what if your salary is **far** lower than that of the role you are applying for?

It shouldn't matter, really, but it can put employers off. They may think you are actually not up to the role, or that you are trying to make a big 'step up'. Unfortunately, they may discount your application if there is too big a gap, and not read the CV to discover that you *are* a good candidate.

Ways round the problem:

◆ Explain! If your role was a training role, or you were promised a pay rise which never materialised, consider whether a simple honest explanation would be a good idea.

◆ Add a reassuring sentence to ensure they know you are capable.

    e.g.   Although my current role is less well remunerated, my experience to date makes me well prepared for a role such as this, and very capable of carrying out your stated requirements.

◆ List the salary in as 'played up' a form as you can – never list basic salary, you could include bonuses and overtime. Don't lie, but make the figures sound better.

◆ List package rather than salary. This will make the number seem larger.

◆ Don't list the salary, in case it puts them off your CV. If you have to, give the salary at the bottom of your CV on the last page. They will have read your CV and judged your suitability before they come to it.

◆ Omit the salary – altogether.

In summary...

◆ Write a professional looking covering letter to enhance your CV, not repeat it.

◆ Make sure it contains enough to get your application noticed – the object is to get the CV read and given full consideration.

◆ Let them know you are aware of the company, what it does and how you can fit in.

◆ Never give your salary unless forced to.

Chapter 5

Checking and Sending the CV

In this Chapter:

- ◆ **analysing the advert or job description**
- ◆ **tailoring everything to the job**
- ◆ **proofreading**
- ◆ **electronic CVs**
- ◆ **faxing/scanning CVs.**

Once the CV is right, and the covering letter is good, you have to get them to the employer in a format they can easily work with.

Now that you have a good CV and covering letter, you have to get them to the employer. It's no longer as simple as sending them by post – many applications can be sent by e-mail, and some employers require this.

Making the finished product perfect, before it leaves your hands, is essential. But **how** you send it is also important in today's electronic world. Documents to be e-mailed need preparation before sending, to ensure they can be opened and read when they arrive. Faxes need similar treatment.

You can't really rely on a kind employer calling you, or replying to tell you that your CV has arrived but they can't read it. Some of them are just too busy, with hundreds of applications coming in weekly in large companies. Careful preparation can make sure your precious details arrive safely, and can be read and judged on their own merits.

Is this you?

❓ *I usually just send my CV by post – with the covering letter of course. Do I really need to change now?*

❓ *It'll cost me a fortune to get fancy card envelopes for all my applications.*

❓ *If they give an e-mail address, surely I can just e-mail the CV as an attachment?*

❓ *Why do they have to make it so complicated? If it takes that long to apply, I could send out three normal letters and CVs in the same time.*

Analysing the advert or job description

If you have an advertisement or job description for the role you are applying for, this is a wealth of information you can use to make sure your covering letter and the CV are made relevant to the job. The advice in this section is relevant to both your CV and covering letter – you want to pick out the available information and make sure you use it to your best advantage.

It may be time-consuming to edit your covering letter and CV and tailor it for every single application, but this really is an excellent thing to do to make them stand out, and it will maximise your chances of success.

Save, don't rewrite

You don't need to rewrite the entire thing – just take your base covering letter and CV and tailor them for each job. If you save the various versions you create, you will soon have a 'bank' of copies which need minimum editing for similar jobs. This will save you time and effort.

Pick out the main points

The first thing to do is to pick out the main points. What is the main purpose of the job, what type of role is it? Try to get a feel for the overall need of the organisation. This is what you aim to make your covering letter and CV feel like. If the overall wording and phrasing of the advert or job description is about a detail-conscious, process-driven environment, don't send in a CV and covering letter that shows how innovative you are! Your covering letter and CV should have the same feel as the advert and/or job description – so in this case you want to come across as a careful, detailed individual.

Identify specific points

There will usually be points mentioned that the organisation is looking for. Highlight or underline these, and make a quick list of them on a sheet of paper. Try to see which are the most important and put them in that order. This gives you a list of words and phrases that you need to incorporate into the covering letter and CV. Using their terminology is better than using your own and hoping they will see you have what they are looking for!

Tailoring everything to the job

Your final check should be that you have tailored everything to the job.

Anyone can send an off-the-shelf CV. Make yours personal from you to them.

◆ Show you know about the company.

◆ Show your skills and/or experience are relevant.

◆ Specify somewhere that you fit all their requirements.

◆ Address everything to the right person.

◆ Follow their recruitment process – stick to their instructions.

Proofreading

Essential factual checks

◆ Contact information – correct, and up to date.

- ◆ Dates – correct for previous roles.

- ◆ Contact name *and* address of the recipient – correct.

- ◆ Company – spelled correctly.

Detail checks

- ◆ Check spelling.

- ◆ Check punctuation.

- ◆ Check for sense – spellcheckers don't pick up wrong words that are spelled correctly; for example, 'check smelling' would be just as acceptable to a spellchecker as 'check spelling'.

- ◆ Check grammar – most computer packages have a grammar checker. It may even improve your English in the process!

- ◆ Check spacing is consistent between headings.

- ◆ CV layout – good spacing, etc.

- ◆ Active language throughout.

- ◆ Never fold the CV unless absolutely necessary. Your aim is for it to arrive pristine and neat.

Check for quality of information

- ◆ Describe your accomplishments as well as your duties.

- ◆ Check you've told them how you fit their requirements.

- ◆ Check for negatives – rephrase or rewrite as positives

wherever possible.

- Highlight key points if necessary.

- Check all information supplied is honest and factual.

- Do not state salary information unless this is absolutely essential.

Get help

- Find someone else to check your work once it's completed.

- Get help with grammar if necessary.

- Get input on layout – do they like it? Improvements?

The CV and covering letter are two documents that can literally change your life. They could have more impact on your finances than almost anything else. So invest time in making sure they are as good as possible.

Electronic CVs

If you have an e-mail address to send an application to, it can save you time and money – and prevent postal services delaying, losing or crumpling your CV.

But there is little point in using e-mail if your beautifully crafted CV comes out as sheets of garbage at the other end. Highlighting, bold type, paragraphing – all may get distorted and make your CV hard to read.

To impress employers using e-mail or the Internet for recruitment, send them the CV in your usual, word-processed format, and also send a copy in a format they can read, which will come out at the other end as you intended. The two main formats are ASCII format and RTF format. Use ASCII format if the format style of the CV is not important. If you want to preserve some of the style, use RTF format.

For absolute certainty, you should always send an e-mail with two versions of the CV as attachments, one word-processed and one RTF or ASCII, stating you have done this for ease of reference.

RTF format CVs

These can be viewed by most word processors. They retain paragraphs, page formatting, and the physical appearance of the document.

◆ Save the CV as a rich text file (RTF format).

◆ Send the CV as an attachment

◆ Write your covering letter as the e-mail text, not as a separate attachment.

◆ Say in the e-mail that your attachment is RTF format – these can be reliably read by most word processors.

◆ It is best never to cut and paste your CV into the bottom of the e-mail itself – this simply makes your e-mail appear very long and messy.

e.g.   Never say "In case you have any difficulty opening or reading my attachment, I have pasted a copy of the text of my CV at the bottom of this e-mail."

ASCII format CVs

ASCII files are text only files which are universally recognisable. They contain punctuation, spaces, etc., but no formatting information. They are used for two main reasons. Firstly, they can be used by non-PC machines such as Macintoshes or UNIX workstations. Secondly, they can easily be saved into an electronic database for searching (see later).

◆ Only ever use ASCII format if asked for it. RTF files are far more widely used nowadays.

◆ Check the CV has only 6.5 inches of text per line. This will prevent 'scrolling' of text onto new lines, which looks messy.

◆ Use courier typeface – ASCII files usually display using this particular type, so it will help you see your CV as it will come out at the other end.

◆ Remove all formatting – bullets, underlining, italics, bold, quotation marks, etc.

◆ Asterisks, plus signs and minus signs do not get changed in transmission if you *must* use emphasis.

◆ Save the CV as ASCII format.

◆ Attach the file as a 'text only' file to send.

♦ State in the e-mail that your attachment is in ASCII format.

Don't let things stand in the way of your CV being received and used. You need to understand the technology involved just well enough to manipulate it so your work arrives in as good a condition as it was sent.

Faxing/scanning CVs

CVs which are to be **faxed** need special handling. Certain things make it hard to read faxed CVs:

♦ any colour but white paper

♦ non-black text

♦ italics

♦ underlining

♦ small type (never use less than 11 point)

♦ lack of large margins around the edge of each page.

As hundreds of companies are beginning to use technology to assist with their recruitment, they are starting to store candidate CVs electronically, which means **scanning** in their CVs.

> *You may lose out – if a company has to ask you to re-send your CV, the job may already be filled by the time you reply. Get it right first time.*

The same rules apply to **scannable CVs** as faxes. But you should also avoid:

◆ indentations

◆ centred text

◆ columns

◆ tables

◆ non-'sans serif' fonts.

Scanned CVs are usually used for **electronic searching** – the company enters keywords of skills and experience they are looking for, and computer programs assess how good a match you are with the job. They then sort candidates and prioritise your application compared to others. If you haven't tailored your CV to the advertised job, you could lose out. It is essential to make sure you have included all the keywords in the advertisement or job description on your CV, so that the program will find them.

CV scanning programs like **nouns** – including noun forms of verbs: purchasing, supervising, administering, interviewing, etc. Use them. You may even need to reword your CV to make allowances for this – add more nouns if necessary.

As more companies start to use technology to fill their vacancies, you need to make your CV usable by that technology, to get your CV considered fully for each appropriate role.

In summary...

◆ Make sure you know enough about the company to know you want to work there, and let them know you have researched this.

◆ Check your CV as many times as necessary to get perfection. Then get someone else to check it.

◆ Understand technology well enough to make sure you can safely send your CV electronically to recruiters.

◆ If your CV is to be faxed or scanned, you will need to allow extra time for amendments to prepare it.

Appendix: Examples

On the following pages you will find examples of covering letters, chronological and functional CVs. They all vary in style – none is perfect (there's no such thing) but any one could be regarded as 'best practice'.

They illustrate a variety of layouts and principles for you.

Josie M Davies
8 Leaves Road
Treetown
Woods
W00 0DY

Mrs J Prestwick
Recruitment Manager
ABC Printing Company
Treetown
Woods
W00 9BB

Dear Mrs Prestwick

Vacancy JP/422 – Administrator, Printing Department
Evening Newspaper 21/1/00

I was interested to read your advertisement for the above
position. I have been looking for a similar role in a growing
organisation to enhance my experience.

I feel I have much to offer, and hope that after considering
my enclosed CV, you will agree that my experience is both
relevant and adequate. For example, I have used all
computer packages listed as requirements for the job.

In particular, my current role at Company A is similar enough
to have provided an excellent background and experience in
audit trails and office administration, but leaves me keen to
progress to a larger team and organisation.

Your role has a focus on quality audit and ABC tracking,
which is always a requirement in the printing industry, but
your expansion plans mean that cost control and quality
issues will be a particular focus for you over the coming year.
I have a great deal of experience in both areas and so would
be excited at the prospect of joining your team at such a
time.

I look forward to hearing from you, and do hope you find
my CV to be of interest.

Yours sincerely

Josie Davies, Mrs

Example of a covering letter

Mrs Jill Godwin
8 Acremead
Devonshire
TN5 8BB

J D Evans
Head of Administration
RJJ Bank
15 High Street
London
EC89 5JJ

1 March 200X

Dear Sir

Application – Secretarial Work

I have recently returned from a year's visit to the USA, and am looking for a suitable secretarial opportunity. I have enclosed my CV for your attention, and would hope that you find my details of interest.

My previous work in London was not in banking, but I am confident that my secretarial skills are appropriate to a banking environment, as my last role at JD Wills and Partners (a law firm) was as team secretary to a small team of partners working with banking clients.

Owing to my circumstances, I am available immediately, and would be delighted to discuss my CV with you, should you think this would be helpful.

I look forward to hearing from you.

Yours sincerely

Jill Godwin, Mrs

Example of a covering letter on a speculative basis

KATHERINE JACOB

42 Oaktree Avenue, Bedlam, Cheshire CC3 333
Mobile: 0976 000000

PROFILE:

A multi-skilled 'all-rounder' with excellent interpersonal and administrative skills, seeking an administration role.

KEY SKILLS/EXPERIENCE:

- Efficient administration, combined with attention to detail – ensuring the smooth running of a Company Training Division
- Excellent co-ordination skills – e.g. managed the successful completion of nation-wide training projects
- Strong interpersonal and client care skills – e.g. awarded internal company 'Client Care' Award

IT SKILL SET:

- Windows, Microsoft Word, Excel, PowerPoint, Lotus Notes, cc:Mail, MS Mail, the Internet

EDUCATION:

St Joseph's School   1978–1985
- O Levels: 11
- A Levels: English (A), History (A), Economics (B)

Devon University, BA (Hons) Geography   1986–1990

Example of a chronological CV (page 1 of 2)

EMPLOYMENT DETAILS:

Various temporary short-term assignments Oct 1999 – Present
Secretary/Administrator (Temporary)

Training Company plc
Training Account Manager   *Mar 1998 – Oct 1999*

- Identified/developed training opportunities within existing company Accounts
- Responsible for all training issues including the pricing of training and its successful delivery
- Managed nation-wide tailored training programmes
- Liaised with 3rd Party suppliers to secure preferential rates for customers while maximising margin
- Exceeded each Quarter Sales Target

Complc Computer Training
Account Manager   *June 1996 – Mar 1998*

- Established and developed client base for new Manchester training centre
- Identified/sold scheduled and tailored IT training solutions to businesses
- Managed contracts for 50 staff, involving close liaison with other Departments

Independent Computer Solutions
Training Administrator   *May 1991 – June 1996*

- Organised courses, trainers and facilities for all scheduled, company specific and onsite training projects
- Established administrative systems to maximise departmental efficiency
- Organised marketing activities, including direct mail campaigns, writing promotional materials
- Monitored performance against targets

Example of a chronological CV (page 2 of 2)

Example of a CV combining functional and chronological elements –for an IT professional where it can be useful to use a functional section to indicate IT software and/or hardware expertise.

STEVEN JENKINS

ADDRESS   8 Brook Lane
                     Readford RD7 7DD
PHONE   079 12044-1298
EMAIL ADDRESS   SJ@sj.co.uk
DATE OF BIRTH   16 February 1973

QUALIFICATIONS   Bachelor of Computing & Mathematical
                     Sciences, Information Systems, Herriot
                     University, Vancouver 1996 (1st class)

A motivated and reliable person who believes in the highest standards of excellence and personal achievement. Experienced in IT solutions for a variety of business areas, providing more accurate and timely information, cost savings and improving communication and data requirements.

SPECIFIC IT EXPERIENCE

4+ years	ADO / OLE DB, ODBC
	MS Access, DAO, VBA
	MS Excel, VBA including OLE code
	RDBMS – Analysis & Design (data-flow
	diagrams, design documentation)
3–4 years	SQL Server 7 / 2000, Transact-SQL
	Visual Basic & COM
2–3 years	Windows NT
1–2 years	HTML
	Sybase Adaptive Server V12
	Unix
0–6 months	ASP, VB Script
	Formal testing (structural, link, functional)

WORK EXPERIENCE
Jan 03 – Aug 03 Travel
May 01 – Dec 02 JP JAMES – London, Analyst/Programmer (CONTRACT)
- Developed, supported and managed applications within Front and Middle Offices.
- Provided tactical cost-effective solutions in a fast-changing business environment

---

Example of a CV combining functional and chronological elements
(page 1 of 2)

- Liaised and oversaw the IT interests of the department including future requirements and daily support.
- Setup standard procedures for support and development including system and user documentation.
- Achieved huge time savings and increased accuracy in capturing new transactions.
- Time efficiency increased from 2 weeks to 2 days for confirmation.
- Improved confirmation tracking, no lost transactions, automated generation of confirmations.

Jun 00 – Apr 01   Travelling

Mar 99 – Jun 00   JP JAMES – London, Analyst/ Programmer (CONTRACT)
- Developed a database to maximize the benefits of the new IT architecture.
- Consolidated profit at instrument level and calculated an accurate funding figure.
- ½ day saved through automatic verification of data for completeness and accuracy.
- Predicted variance caused by system methodology differences.
- Successful implementation realizing efficiency gains and a very high level of control.

Feb 98 – Mar 99   SMS Systems UK Ltd, Test Analyst/ Programmer
- Designed database solution to produce user-defined ad-hoc reports from the company's SQL accounting database.
- Conducted formal testing (structural, link and functional) of MS Access databases used to check and migrate data from existing database systems to SAP.
- Tested compliance against System Design Specification and Program Specification documents.

Aug 96 – Jun 99   Readchester City Council, Analyst/ Programmer
- Developed and supported the 1st line customer support and sales database for business refuse.
- Conducted a historical sales analysis leading to a monthly sales increase by 15%
- Instigated performance tuning to aid 1st line support and maintain head count with higher sales volumes.
- The solutions equated to a £50k/yr saving by providing a more accurate picture of their data in a timely manner.

Example of a CV combining functional and chronological elements
(page 2 of 2)

LESLEY GOSS
2 Garden Street
London EW1 2QJ

08996 549726
SOLAINE@hotmail.co.uk

BILINGUAL RECEPTIONIST/CUSTOMER SERVICES
Excellent presentation combined with experienced customer service within a Reception environment. Committed to work in a fast pace with a mature approach.

WORK EXPERIENCE
Jun 2001 – present   **LETTINGS INTERNATIONAL AGENCY – London**
Receptionist /Switchboard
- Running reception of a deluxe property company
- Answering switchboard and allocating calls
- Informing members of staff by email about packages or appointments
- Supporting administration within the letting office and helping with foreign language queries
- Ensure full payments taken and signature of Tenancy Agreement
- Ensure departure's date with guests and dealing with invoice manually
- Signing departure key's books and registered in book from letting
- Viewing apt by appointment and dealing with invoice from letting.

Jun 2000 – May 2001 PERFECTION HOTEL – London
Receptionist/Cashier
- Working within a busy environment in a 4*star Hotel
- Check in/check out guests and refund guests when overcharged
- Responsible on a daily basic of all incoming cash within the hotel
- Supporting events team for exhibitions, weddings etc
- Exchanging foreign monies for guests – cashier, petty cash and banking for hotel

Dec 1999 – Jun. 2000 EDEN PLAZA HOTEL – London
Receptionist
- Working in a small hotel located in central London
- Responsible daily for reservations and cash handling
- Check in or check out guests and arranging wake up call on switchboard

Example of simple chronological CV (page 1 of 2)

Aug 1999 – Dec 1999 ROCHESTER HOTEL – London
                              Trainee Receptionist
- Answering calls and allocating on ISDX switchboard
- Booking reservation face to face or by phone on system
- Counting float and banking. Backed up data daily
- Checked in or check out guests

EDUCATION AND TRAINING COURSES

Jan 2002 – Oct 2002   Microsoft Word (Beginner to Advance)
                          Microsoft Excel (Beginner to Advance)
Feb 1999 – Aug 1999   **CALLENDAR COLLEGE – London**
                          Business Admin NVQ (Level I II)

Jan 1996 – Jun 1999   **WESTMINSTER COLLEGE – London**
                          English Course at Higher Intermediate level
                          Training Course in Microsoft Word
                          GSCE Equivalent (10 subjects)
                          Spanish, English, Math, History, French, Geography, Biology, Economics, Art, Sport

PERSONAL INTERESTS
LANGUAGES   French (native), English (bilingual), Spanish (Basic)
IT Skills   Good knowledge in Word, Excel, (basic Access)
Hobbies   Reading, Tapestry, History,
Sport   Swimming, Jogging, Cycling, Badminton

Example of simple chronological CV (page 2 of 2)

JILL GODWIN

8 Acremead   **01456-788199**
Devonshire
TN5 8BB

Jill@godwin.co.uk

EDUCATION

James Street Comprehensive   3 A levels
1968–1973   11 O levels

Gordonwell College, Rotherhampton   Secretarial Diploma
1973–1974   Typing speed, 80 wpm
                                      Shorthand

EMPLOYMENT HISTORY

Nov 1999 –   Accompanied husband to USA on business
Jan 2001

Jan 1992 –   **JD Wills and Partners –** *Team Secretary, banking*
              team
Oct 1999   • Working with 6 partners in banking team
              • Organising meetings, diary management, client
                liaison, etc.
              • Full organisation of client functions,
                presentations, and associated event
                management
              • Preparation of all client documentation,
                including reports and detailed summaries of
                discussions
              • Active member of firm's social committee

July 1987 –   Full-time parent (three children)
Jan 1992

Oct 1983   **Evans Associates –** *Secretary to Finance Manager*
July 1987   • Full secretarial support to Finance Manager of
                busy engineering company headquarters
              • Handling all correspondence
              • Assistance in preparation of management
                reports, annual report etc.
              • Supervisor of headquarters receptionist

Example of a chronological CV with gaps (page 1 of 2)

March 1979	**J P Publishing – *Typing Pool Supervisor***
Oct 1983	• Joined typing pool and was promoted to supervisor in 1981
	• Management of all workloads
	• Supervision of 4 typing pool staff
	• Arrangement of temporary cover for sickness absence etc.
	• Provision of temporary cover for reception and management PAs

Oct 1974	**Silverwood Management Consultants – *Secretary***
March 1979	***receptionist***
	• Receptionist, meeting and greeting all clients and visitors
	• Secretarial support to senior managers
	• Deputising for PAs of senior management team during holidays/sickness
	• Handling all mail in and out, plus all couriers, deliveries etc.

Example of a chronological CV with gaps (page 2 of 2)

NAME: John Manors

AGE: 58

EDUCATION:
1955 – 1960   Treeborough Technical College
Accountancy and Financial Management
course

CAREER SUMMARY:

Apr 1997 – to date   **INDEPENDENT FINANCE** – *Financial Consultant*

Duties:
- Responsible for setting up accounting systems
- Checking all transactions, interest and cash balances

Jan 1991 – Mar 1997   **FYR LTD** – *Chief Finance Officer*

Duties:
- Set up company on behalf of parent company
- Responsible for arranging all financial registrations, finding premises, arranging lease, installing computer systems and purchasing/leasing all equipment necessary to run a new company
- Completely 'hands on' role responsible for every function of a financial nature
- All accounting functions
- Responsible for monthly reporting, production of daily/monthly/annual reports
- Liaison with clients, reconciliation and payments where necessary
- Payment to all suppliers
- Management team member for company staff of 19

Example CV – chronological, covering a long time period
(page 1 of 2)

| 1985 – 1991 | **INDUSTRIAL PLUMBING CO** – |
| | *Management Accountant* |

Duties:
- Production of daily/weekly/monthly reports
- Production of daily profit and loss accounts for London, Bristol and Leeds profit centres
- Balancing of financial controls
- Authorisation and release of all company payments via electronic banking systems
- Reporting over limits to the Credit Director

| 1978 – 1991 | **E & F LTD** |

Position: Operations Manager

Duties:
- Responsible for the direct reporting to the treasurer for all financial transactions
- Management of 3 staff producing daily reconciliations

| 1960 – 1978 | **VARIOUS ROLES** |

- Management and accounting positions

Example CV – chronological, covering a long time period
(page 2 of 2)

JERRY EVANS-COTTRELL

22 Mortimer Road
London
NS4 6DA

020-75689-2563

PROFILE
A hard working and numerate accounts professional with a positve and motivated approach. Able to organise and prioritise workloads in order to meet strict deadlines. A good team player but also works well on own initiative keeping a cool and focused head under pressure. A stong communicator, used to dealing with people at all levels. Currently studying for CIMA. Flexible regarding working hours and happy to travel within the UK and Europe.

EXPERIENCE

October 2002 to present Fox Temps Ltd – London
- Bank reconciliations
- Handling wages control and journals for both temporary staff and monthly payroll
- Keeping sales and purchase ledger updated
- Nominal ledger reconciliations (PAYE, Inland revenue control a/cs etc)
- Credit control (up to litigation stage) and handling of clients accounting queries
- Assisting auditors at year end
- Various other ad hoc reporting (Excel) as required ie Year End Wages & Salaries reports etc.

November 2001-April 2002 Reynolds Accountants – London
Accounts Assistant (temp contract)
- Credit control
- Managing of accounts up to £50,000
- Sales, purchase and nominal ledger
- Bank reconciliations
- Bank cashiering duties
- Assisting company executives in preparation of all accounting documentation
- Dealing with vendor payment administration.

Example of a chronological CV (page 1 of 2)

EDUCATION
- Currently studying (part time) CIMA (currently finishing Foundation level, commencing Intermediate level in August 2003)
- HND Business Studies (Caterham College of Technology 1998-1999)
- HNC Business Administration (Sowerwell College of Commerce, 1997-1998)
- GNVQ Business Administration (Sowerwell College, 1996-1997)
- GCSE's (all grades 2-3) German, English, Mathematics, History, Chemistry, Computing Studies, Religious Education.

IT KNOWLEGE
Sage, Word, Powerpoint, Excel, Adapt, FacFlow (factoring software), Bankline, BACS, Outlook.

INTERESTS
Reading

Example of a chronological CV (page 2 of 2)

CURRICULUM VITAE – MICHAEL EVANS

MICHAEL (MIKE) EVANS   Home phone. 01234 098 7654
99 Leaves Road   Mobile No. 07999 123123
Treetown
Woods
W00 0DY

E-mail Mike@emailprovider.co.uk

PERSONAL PROFILE

A lively, enthusiastic and confident graduate with excellent interpersonal, organisational and analytical skills. Keen to progress and develop a career in management – on a graduate or management training programme. Self-assured with the ability to work as a team member or under own initiative. Able to work conscientiously, methodically, and to strict deadlines, maintaining high standards of work.

EDUCATION

1990–1997   ***Highmere Comprehensive, Treetown***
GCSEs   x 10 subjects
A levels in   French, Spanish and Geography

Treetown University
BA in Interpreting and Translation (French and Spanish) – Grade 2.1

CORE SKILLS

IT Skills

Windows 95 and 98, Lotus 123, Excel

Communication Skills

Good natural communicator, practised in giving presentations. Communication abilities were developed and tested at University through the degree course. For example, concise relaying of information between parties requiring translation has facilitated development of high standards of

Example of a functional CV (page 1 of 2)

communication and verbal reasoning. Liaison, conferencing and simultaneous interpreting have involved the ability to maintain calm at all times, plus the ability to think quickly and rationally under pressure.

Organisational Skills

During the year spent working abroad as part of the degree course, organisation skills were tested. There was a requirement to write a dissertation in both languages, which made organisation essential. Carrying out detailed research was necessary. In particular, this research involved arranging, preparing and conducting interviews with individuals with experience relevant to the topic. It was also necessary to ensure interviews yielded useful information. Other factors, such as arrangement of my own travel and accommodation arrangements, developed my confidence during this time.

Interpersonal Skills

During the year abroad, time was spent teaching English in France. This tested my ability to relate to people. Finding new and interesting ways to encourage student participation in classes demanded creativity and a friendly, approachable manner. Vacation employment in the last three years has required a more formal professional approach, by contrast. Saturday work at SSS Newsagents also necessitated a high degree of teamwork and interpersonal transactions, which developed my skills in this area.

WORK EXPERIENCE

1998 – Present **Chartered Accountants Company, Treetown**
Vacation employment

Duties included receptionist, word processing, correspondence and preliminary work preparing financial accounts. Some involvement with clients.

1991–1996 **SSS Newsagents, Treetown**
Saturday Sales Assistant

Duties included selling, till operation, customer service, dealing with suppliers and other branches.

Example of a functional CV (page 2 of 2)